GUINNESS WORLD RECORDS

ULTIMATE GROSS RECORDS

COLLECT & COMPARE WITH

FEARLESS FEATS
Incredible Records of Human Achievement

WILD LIVES
Outrageous Animal & Nature Records

JUST OUTRAGEOUS!
Extraordinary Records of Unusual Facts & Feats

DEADLY DISASTERS
Catastrophic Records in History

MYSTERIES & MARVELS OF THE PAST
Historical Records of Phenomenal Discoveries

BIGGEST, TALLEST, GREATEST!
Records of Overwhelming Size

BOOK OF ULTIMATE RECORDS

EXTREME ANIMALS!

ULTIMATE PET RECORDS

GUINNESS WORLD RECORDS

ULTIMATE GROSS RECORDS

Compiled by Kris Hirschmann and Ryan Herndon

For Guinness World Records:
Jennifer Gilmour, Stephen Fall,
Craig Glenday, Stuart Claxton, Michael Whitty,
and Laura Nieberg

SCHOLASTIC INC.

NEW YORK   TORONTO   LONDON   AUCKLAND   SYDNEY
MEXICO CITY   NEW DELHI   HONG KONG

Attempting to break records or set new records can be dangerous. Appropriate advice should be taken first, and all record attempts are undertaken entirely at the participant's risk. In no circumstances will Guinness World Records Limited or Scholastic Inc. have any liability for death or injury suffered in any record attempts. Guinness World Records Limited has complete discretion over whether or not to include any particular records in the annual *Guinness World Records* book.

Guinness World Records Limited has a very thorough accreditation system for records verification. However, while every effort is made to ensure accuracy, Guinness World Records Limited cannot be held responsible for any errors contained in this work. Feedback from our readers on any point of accuracy is always welcomed.

© 2011 Guinness World Records Limited

No part of this work may be reproduced, stored in a retrieval system, or transmitted in any form or by any means, electronic, mechanical, photocopying, recording, or otherwise, without written permission of the publisher. For information regarding permission, write to Scholastic Inc., Attention: Permissions Department, 557 Broadway, New York, NY 10012.

Published by Scholastic Inc. SCHOLASTIC and associated logos are trademarks and/or registered trademarks of Scholastic Inc.

ISBN 978-0-545-30851-9

Designed by Henry Ng
Photo Research by Els Rijper
Records from the Archives of Guinness World Records

12 11 10 9 8 7 6 5 4 3 2 1   11 12 13 14 15 16/0

Printed in the U.S.A.   40

First printing, September 2011

Visit Guinness World Records at **www.guinnessworldrecords.com**

CONTENTS

The idea for Guinness World Records grew out of a question. In 1951, Sir Hugh Beaver, the managing director of the Guinness Brewery, wanted to know which was the fastest game bird in Europe — the golden plover or the grouse? Some people argued that it was the grouse. Others claimed it was the plover. A book to settle the debate did not exist until Sir Hugh discovered the knowledgeable twin brothers Norris and Ross McWhirter, who lived in London.

Like their father and grandfather, the McWhirter twins loved information. They were kids when they started clipping interesting facts from newspapers and memorizing important dates in world history. As well as learning the names of every river, mountain range, and nation's capital, they knew the record for pole squatting (196 days in 1954), which language had only one irregular verb (Turkish), and that the grouse — flying at a timed speed of 43.5 miles per hour — is faster than the golden plover at 40.4 miles per hour.

Norris and Ross served in the Royal Navy during World War II, graduated from college, and launched their own fact-finding business called McWhirter Twins, Ltd. They were the perfect people to compile the book of records that Sir Hugh Beaver searched for yet could not find.

The first edition of *The Guinness Book of Records* was published on August 27, 1955, and since then has been published in 25 languages and more than 100 countries. In 2000, the book title changed to *Guinness World Records* and has set an incredible record of its own: Excluding non-copyrighted books such as the Bible and the Koran, *Guinness World Records* is the best-selling book of all time!

Today, the official Keeper of the Records keeps a careful eye on each Guinness World Record, compiling and verifying the greatest the world has to offer — from the fastest and the tallest to the slowest and the smallest, with everything in between.

INTRODUCTION
Grossed Out

For more than 50 years, Guinness World Records has measured, weighed, timed, verified, and documented the world's record-breakers in every category imaginable. Today, the records in their archives number more than 40,000.

This book features 46 of the smelliest, slimiest, and most shocking records set by animals, plants, and people. Whether it is a slime-sneezing fish or an eyeball-popping woman, these record-holders earned their place in history with their astonishing abilities. Some people may find the results "gross," but the differences between us are what makes the world such an interesting and exciting place to explore.

Do you think you can handle measuring the loudest burp? Could your nose withstand the smelliest flower or frog? These records and dozens of others — including a nearly headless yet healthy chicken — await YOU in this record-setting gross-out collection!

CHAPTER 1
Weird Skills

Guinness World Record-breakers discover their talents by daring to answer the question, "Can I do it?" They keep their special skills sharp through steady practice. In this chapter, you'll meet people with unusual abilities, ranging from milk-squirters to spaghetti-sneezers, but we don't guarantee they would be everyone's choice for dinnertime entertainment!

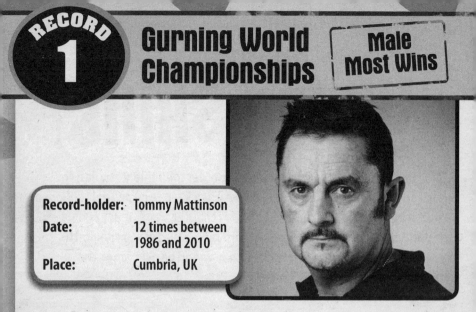

Record-holder:	Tommy Mattinson
Date:	12 times between 1986 and 2010
Place:	Cumbria, UK

Since you will be making many grossed-out faces while reading this book, you could start your training in gurning, the art of making grotesque faces. The Gurning World Championship is held in Cumbria, UK, during the Egremont Crab Fair, which was founded in 1267 to celebrate the area's harvest of crab apples. People's funny faces made after tasting the tart fruit became a popular sport. Tommy Mattinson of Aspatria, Cumbria, has taken the top prize home 12 times to set the record for **Gurning World Championships — Male — Most Wins** (pictured showing his normal face and gurning face). Tommy won in 1986 and 1987, then 10 times more between 1999 and 2010. This weird skill runs in Tommy's family because the previous 10-time champion was Gordon Mattinson, his father!

ULTIMATE FACTS!

The record for **Gurning World Championships — Female — Most Wins** belongs to Anne Woods with 27 wins between 1977 and 2010 at the Egremont Crab Fair in Cumbria, UK.

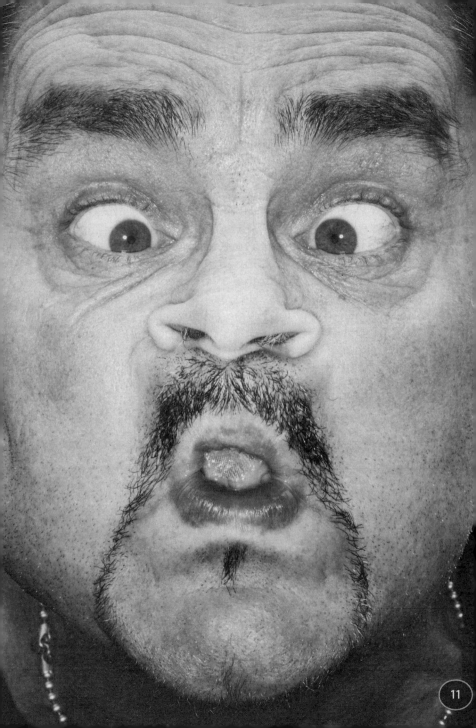

Many people push their limits to set a Guinness World Record, but they must follow safety precautions during their attempts. When Garry Turner of Caistor, UK, went head-to-head against record-challenger Teofilo of Spain, Garry knew two things: He had a special ability to go beyond the limits and he only needed one more clothespin to break his old record for **Most Clothespins Clipped on a Face** (pictured). Garry has Ehlers-Danlos Syndrome, a rare medical condition, making the skin more elastic. He was able to handle his face's skin being pinched and pulled more than Teofilo, who managed to clip almost 140 clothespins to his face before giving up. Garry clipped 160 clothespins to set the new record on the set of Guinness World Records TV show in Madrid, Spain, on January 9, 2009.

ULTIMATE FACTS!

Garry Turner is a dual record-holder! He set his other record of **Stretchiest Skin** by pulling the skin of his stomach to a length of 6.25 inches during the Guinness World Records: Primetime TV show in Los Angeles, California, on October 29, 1999.

Record-holder: Garry Turner
Date: January 9, 2009
Place: Madrid, Spain

Fastest Sandwich Made Using Feet

Record-holder:	Rob Williams
Date:	November 10, 2000
Place:	California, USA

Would you like some jam with your lunch — TOE jam, that is? This extra-icky condiment made it onto the menu on November 10, 2000, when Rob Williams of Austin, Texas, used his feet to assemble a sandwich in just 1 minute and 57 seconds on the set of *Guinness World Records: Primetime* in Los Angeles, California. That's the **Fastest Sandwich Made Using Feet** (pictured)! The toe-rrific treat consisted of two slices of bread, bologna, slices of square, processed cheese, lettuce, tomatoes, mustard, mayonnaise, and pickles. Even more impressively, Rob had to use his talented toes to open and remove all the packaging, peel off the rinds, plus slice the tomatoes and pickles. Now *that's* what we call a real foot-long sandwich!

ULTIMATE FACTS

A career comedy performer, Rob Williams is famous for his foot-built sandwiches, and so are the people who eat them. Talk show host Jay Leno and singer Donny Osmond are among the many celebrities who have shared the stage and split a sandwich with Rob.

Longest Burp

Record-holder:	Michele Forgione
Date:	June 16, 2009
Place:	Reggiolo, Italy

Mi scusi! That means "excuse me" in Italian. We certainly hope these words are well known to Italy's Michele Forgione, who holds the Guinness World Record for the **Longest Burp** (pictured). Michele, who goes by the nickname "Rutt Mysterio" ("Mysterious Belch"), achieved this title on June 16, 2009, by belching continually for 1 minute, 13 seconds, and 57 milliseconds. The marathon emission occurred in Reggiolo, Italy, during the 13th annual Hard Rock "Ruttosound" competition. Thousands of fans showed up to witness the record-breaking burp, and that's no surprise — they knew the contest would be a total *gas!*

ULTIMATE FACTS!

The scientific term for burping is **eructation**. A burp happens when gas escapes from the digestive tract through the mouth. It often causes rude sounds and odors. What did you eat for lunch? Your burps tell the tale!

Loudest Burp

Record-holders:	Elisa Cagnoni (female) and Paul Hunn (male)
Dates:	June 16, 2009, and August 23, 2009
Place:	Reggiolo, Italy, and Bognor Regis, UK

For maximum disgust-o-power, a burp shouldn't just be *loooong*. It should be LOUD, too — and these two record-holders really know how to pump up the volume! The ladies' title for **Loudest Burp** goes to Elisa Cagnoni of Italy, who stunned the Ruttosound crowd with a belch of 107.0 decibels (dB) on June 16, 2009. That's about the same volume as a lawn mower revving up three feet away from your ears, *ouch!* Yet Elisa's ear-splitting emission can't match the level of the male burp, produced by expert belcher Paul Hunn (pictured) at Butlins, Bognor Regis, UK, on August 23, 2009. Measuring an incredible 109.9 decibels, Paul's belch undoubtedly rattled the windows and the eardrums of everyone present.

ULTIMATE FACTS!

What do Paul Hunn's family members think of his incredible burping talent? "My dad used to be disgusted by it, but now I think he is secretly proud. My daughter ... is showing great promise. I think it's great and want to encourage her, but her mum is less impressed," Paul laughed in a 2008 interview.

Let 'Er Rip!

The word *Ruttosound* means "Belch Sounds." It's not a fancy title, but no one can deny its accuracy! The annual Ruttosound competition, which is held in the town of Reggiolo, Italy, pits the world's best burpers against each other in a gross-but-giggle-inducing gas-off. Originally organized to raise money for charity, the event has become more popular every year and now boasts an estimated 30,000 attendees. Despite this success, don't look for Ruttosound footage on the local news. City officials tolerate the event but refuse to embrace it. "They don't want Reggiolo to be identified as the 'Belch City.' So we try to be discreet," explains an event organizer.

Farthest Eyeball Pop

Record-holder: Kim Goodman
Date: November 2, 2007
Place: Istanbul, Turkey

You won't believe your eyes when you see this record-holder in action! Kim Goodman of Chicago, Illinois, has the rare ability to push her eyeballs partway out of their sockets. She discovered this talent in 1992, when she "popped" her eyes by accident. Unharmed and unafraid, Kim has been sharing her eye-opening skills on TV shows, in commercials, and through other media ever since. Kim's crowning achievement occurred in Istanbul, Turkey, on November 2, 2007, when she popped her eyeballs a full 0.47 inches beyond her eye sockets — breaking her own record set in 1998 of the **Farthest Eyeball Pop** ever measured (pictured). Congratulations and here's looking at you, kid!

Heaviest Weight Pulled with the Eye Sockets

Record-holder:	Chayne Hultgren
Date:	April 25, 2009
Place:	Milan, Italy

Australian street artist Chayne Hultgren, who performs under the title "The Space Cowboy," has an interesting *hook* to his act. On April 25, 2009, Chayne inserted a metal hook into each eye socket on the set of TV show *Lo Show dei Record* in Milan, Italy. Attaching the hooks to chains, he used this apparatus to tow a rickshaw filled with three passengers — a total weight of 907 pounds — across the studio floor to set the Guinness World Record for **Heaviest Weight Pulled with the Eye Sockets** (pictured). Chayne also holds the record for **Most Swords Simultaneously Swallowed by a Male**, using 18 swords and performed in Martin Place, Sydney, Australia, on February 8, 2010.

ULTIMATE FACTS!

In one of his most spectacular acts, Chayne swallows a lit fluorescent tube. The bulb glows brightly enough to illuminate his internal organs, which he proudly displays for the audience's amazement.

Dong Changsheng

No Weigh!

The use of untraditional body parts to lift and pull objects is a Guinness World Records staple. Here are some hefty examples:

• Dong Changsheng of China used ropes hooked to his lower eyelids to tow a car weighing 3,307 pounds. Dong set the record for **Heaviest Vehicle Pulled by Eyelids** (pictured).

• Thomas Blackthorne earned many records involving sword-swallowing. He also set the record for **Heaviest Weight Lifted by Tongue** by holding a 27-pound, 8.9-ounce weight latched on a hook pierced through his tongue (pictured). Icky yet impressive — that's another way to make history!

Thomas Blackthorne

Most Balloons Inflated by the Nose in Three Minutes

When it comes to blowing up balloons, Andrew Dahl of the USA wins by a nose! More correctly, by both nostrils. Andrew discovered he had a special talent. He could inflate balloons using his nostrils, not his mouth, and he could use his left and right nostril at the same time. That's two balloons for each exhalation! On March 18, 2010, he put his talent to the test by nasally inflating 23 balloons within the time limit on the set of *Lo Show dei Record* in Rome, Italy. He had to tie all the balloons himself to earn the title of **Most Balloons Inflated by the Nose in Three Minutes** (pictured). See the extra fact note to find out how many balloons he can inflate in 60 minutes!

ULTIMATE FACTS!

Andrew Dahl is a dual record-holder! He earned his first record of **Most Balloons Inflated by the Nose in One Hour** by nasally inflating 308 balloons during the *Live with Regis & Kelly* TV show in New York City, New York, on September 16, 2008.

Record-holder:	Andrew Dahl
Date:	March 18, 2010
Place:	Rome, Italy

Farthest Milk Squirting Distance

Record-holder:	Ilker Yilmaz
Date:	September 1, 2004
Place:	Istanbul, Turkey

Most people prefer to drink milk rather than squirt it out of their nose or eye, but sometimes milk-squirting happens on purpose after hours of practice. On September 1, 2004, Turkish construction worker Ilker Yilmaz poured milk into his hand, snorted it up his nose then ejected the liquid 9 feet 2 inches out of his left eye to earn the title for **Farthest Milk Squirting Distance** (pictured). The ocular ejection took place at the Armada Hotel in Istanbul, Turkey, and was sponsored by a Turkish milk company. Ilker was also the first person to set the record for **Fastest Time to Extinguish Five Candles by Squirting Milk from the Eye** in 2 minutes 7 seconds during the TV show *Guinness World Records — El Show de los Records* in Madrid, Spain. What type of milk does Ilker like to "eye squirt"? Skim or semi-skim because full-fat milk clogs his tear ducts.

Most Milkshake Dispensed Through the Nose

Record-holder:	Gary Bashaw, Jr.
Date:	July 26, 2000
Place:	California, USA

Gary Bashaw, Jr., of Barr, West Virginia, also has a unique talent involving milk. On July 26, 2000, television viewers of the show *Guinness World Records: Primetime* in Los Angeles, California, saw Gary mix milk and chocolate powder in his mouth then dispense the chocolate milk mixture out from one of his nostrils. The slimy smoothie weighed in at 1.82 ounces, which is the **Most Milkshake Dispensed Through the Nose.**

ULTIMATE FACTS!

Many people have expelled milk out of their noses by accident. The mishap usually occurs when a milk-drinker gets the giggles. The laughter raises the air pressure inside the person's head, which forces the liquid out of the drinker's nasal passages (see illustration). *Achoo!*

Longest Spaghetti Nasal Ejection

Record-holder: Kevin Cole
Date: December 16, 1998
Place: California, USA

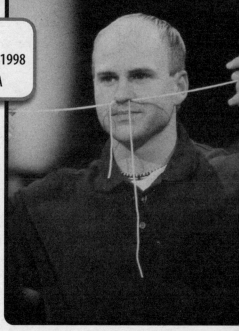

It seems im-PASTA-ble for a person to swallow a noodle then eject it through the nose. But Kevin Cole of Carlsbad, New Mexico, manages this difficult trick with ease! On December 16, 1998, Kevin ate a 7.5-inch strand of spaghetti and blew it out of one nostril to earn the Guinness World Record for **Longest Spaghetti Nasal Ejection** (pictured). To perform the carb-tastic caper, which took place on the set of *Guinness World Records: Primetime* in Los Angeles, California, Kevin used his tongue to push the pasta behind his nasal opening. "Then you just blow," he said. "It's just like blowing your nose." But we advise you to use a tissue, not noodles.

ULTIMATE FACTS!

Kevin Cole prefers to use Ronzoni No. 8 spaghetti noodles for his record attempts. After he ejects one end of a spaghetti strand out of each nostril, he pulls the ends back and forth to create a "nasal floss" effect.

CHAPTER 2
Parasitic Nightmares

Parasites are among Mother Nature's most unsettling creatures. The "bugs" in this chapter are responsible for some of Guinness World Records' creepiest entries in the archives. Turn the page to travel through worm-infested intestines, encounter the thirstiest ticks and leeches, and count 200,000 eggs laid every day by one creature . . . living inside your guts. Time to set some world records by becoming infested!

Largest Sneezing Fish

Record-holder:	Hagfish
Place:	Cold-water oceans worldwide

Gesundheit! You're staring into the sticky mouth of the hagfish or slime eel (*Myxine glutinosa*), which holds the Guinness World Record for **Largest Sneezing Fish** (pictured). One of nature's most repulsive creatures, this primitive and jawless animal gnaws its way into the body of another fish — living, dying, or dead — and chows down on its internal organs. The hagfish then secretes vast amounts of mucus so it can easily slither out of its hollowed-out victim. Feeling a little stuffed up? The hagfish sneezes slime out of its respiratory slits to prevent itself from suffocating in its own mucus.

ULTIMATE FACTS!

To create their slime, hagfish excrete superabsorbent fibers. The fibers are small, but they can trap vast amounts of water — enough to build a ball of goo much larger than the hagfish's body. It takes a hagfish mere minutes to turn a 5-gallon bucket of water into a pool of slime.

Most Bloodthirsty Parasite

Record-holder: Hookworm
Place: Worldwide

Imagine a row of blood-filled gallon jugs that stretches nearly 250 miles. You're looking at the daily diet for the world's population of hookworms (*Anclyostoma duodenale* and *Necator americanus*), the **Most Bloodthirsty Parasite** (pictured). Hookworms infest the intestines of hundreds of thousands of humans, sometimes piling up so thickly that they look like squirming carpets. They're small, slimy, and *hungry*. These parasites enter the human body by boring through the soles of the feet. They travel through the lymphatic system, the body's natural drainage network, into their host's lungs, where they break into the airways. The worms crawl up the windpipe and down the esophagus (food tube) to enter the victim's digestive system. They use sharp mouthparts to pierce their hosts' flesh and suck the blood that spills from the wound — a total of about 2.6 million gallons' worth every day. The legendary human vampire Dracula would be no match for these ravenous bloodsuckers!

Largest Tick

Record-holder:	Hard ticks
Place:	Worldwide

Tick, tick, tick, BOOM! One of the world's most horrifying parasites has an exploding body — figuratively speaking. Members of the hard tick family (*Ixodidae*) start their lives as barely visible specks. The tiny eight-legged arachnids soon attach themselves to warm-blooded hosts and burrow headfirst into their skin. The embedded ticks then drink . . . and drink . . . and drink. Their abdomens swell as hot, fresh blood flows into their systems (pictured). A hard tick may reach a diameter of 1.4 inches before its hunger is satisfied. The **Largest Tick** drops off its host to lay eggs . . . and unleash a whole new tribe of bloodsuckers upon the world.

ULTIMATE FACTS!

Ticks usually hide in tall grasses. They detect nearby animals by body heat and carbon dioxide output. Any animals, including humans, who come near become a mobile meal for the tick that latches on for a free ride.

Sick from a Tick

Ticks aren't just disgusting. They're germy, too, which makes them extra dangerous. In the USA, ticks are responsible for an estimated 95 percent of all animal-borne human infections! The most common of these infections is Lyme disease, which starts as a rash and progresses to arthritis, heart disease, and many other problems. Ticks can also cause Rocky Mountain spotted fever, relapsing fever, encephalitis, and a condition called tick paralysis. To avoid these disorders, you should always cover your arms, legs, and head when you venture into tick-infested areas.

Most Fertile Parasite

Record-holder: Roundworm
Place: Worldwide

What is 18 inches long and lays 200,000 eggs in your belly every day? It sounds like a joke, but it's no laughing matter. These numbers add up to the roundworm, the record-holder for **Most Fertile Parasite** (pictured). One female *Ascaris lumbricoides* can deposit more than 25 million eggs in a human host's gut. This never-ending river of eggs leaves the host's body along with its waste. The eggs find their way into water, soil, and food, where they may become breakfast for a brand-new host.

ULTIMATE FACTS!

The roundworm is the most common human parasite. An estimated 1.4 billion people carry these worms and their eggs in their intestines. In some communities, infection rates reach 100 percent.

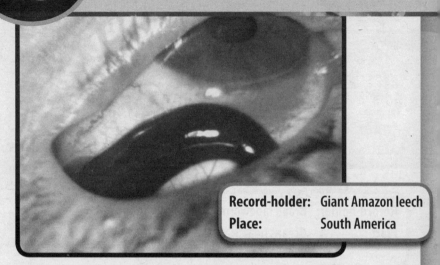

Record-holder:	Giant Amazon leech
Place:	South America

This big bug usually snacks on caimans and snakes, but it will happily dine on *your* blood if it gets the chance! Measuring up to 18 inches in length and nearly 4 inches in width, the giant Amazon leech (*Haementeria ghilianii*) is the **Largest Species of Leech** (pictured). Based on its pictures, it's the *grossest* species, too. Fat, gray, and wrinkled, this sluggish parasite looks like a baby elephant's trunk as it clings, blood-engorged, to its victim's skin. The feeding process is reportedly painless, until you try to remove one from your skin. The leech uses a 6-inch-long retractable tongue like a straw to suck blood from its host.

ULTIMATE FACTS!

The state of New Jersey is the unlikely home of another species of megaleech. First found in 2003, New Jersey's leading leech has an official top length of 17 inches. Unofficial reports, however, claim that the creature may exceed 20 inches. Studies are underway to discover the Guinness World Record-contender's scientific relationships and identity.

Largest Parasite

Record-holder:	Broad tapeworm
Place:	Oceans near Scandinavia, western Russia, and the Baltics

Table for two? You'll need it — or *food* for two, at least — if you unknowingly bring the world's **Largest Parasite** to dinner! The broad or fish tapeworm (*Diphyllobothrium latum*), which inhabits the small intestines of fish and sometimes humans, typically reaches a length of 30 to 40 feet (pictured). A truly impressive specimen, however, can top the 60-foot mark. That's the length of a swimming pool! The human intestine is only about 25 feet long, total, so imagine how bloated you'd feel with this parasitic passenger on board. You'd feel that way for a long time, too, because tapeworms can live up to 20 years!

ULTIMATE FACTS!

The fish tapeworm has several repulsive relatives. The pork tapeworm (*Taenia solium*), which infests humans as well as pigs, can grow longer than 20 feet. And the beef tapeworm (*Taeniarhynchus saginatus*) can be 50 feet long and longer. One extreme specimen measured 75 feet from tip to tip!

CHAPTER 3
Call a Doctor

Sometimes a person will experience a rare disorder or find a unique use for his or her body in the name of scientific learning. Guinness World Records measures, weighs, and writes down the facts behind these stories. Fungal feet, buggy discoveries, and a cheese that will harm your health are under the microscope in this chapter.

Most Dangerous Cheese

Record-holder:	Casu Marzu
Place:	Sardinia, Italy

Normally flies are kept away from food to avoid the risk of contamination. Yet the world's **Most Dangerous Cheese** is made by *allowing* flies to lay eggs inside Pecorino cheese (pictured). The eggs hatch into maggots. The enzymes created by the fly larvae give the finished cheese product a unique taste — but with terrible health effects. This delicacy, known as Casu Marzu or "rotten cheese," is served as a rare treat in Sardinia, Italy. But the still-living maggots can survive stomach acid and pass into the diner's intestine, where they cause vomiting, abdominal pain, and bloody diarrhea. "A mouthful of maggots with every bite!" could be the slogan for Casu Marzu.

ULTIMATE FACTS!

The larvae that live in Casu Marzu can leap 6 inches when disturbed. For this reason, diners often shield their food with their hands to block the maggots' escape.

Most Worms Removed from a Human Stomach

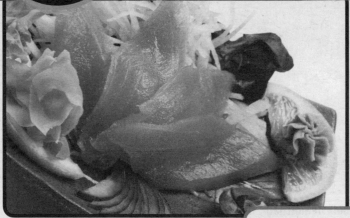

Record-holder:	Anonymous patient
Date:	May 1990
Place:	Shizuoka, Japan

A raw fish-dish from Japan called sashimi (pictured) is popular around the world. It might be a little less popular if people knew it was responsible for the **Most Worms Removed from a Human Stomach**! In May 1990, a 58-year-old woman from Shizuoka, Japan, was admitted to the Isogaki Gastro-Entero-Surgical clinic. The woman had recently eaten a sashimi meal and began complaining of severe gastric pain and nausea. Doctors performed emergency surgery and discovered 56 white, threadlike worms — some measuring up to 0.67 inches long — infesting the patient's stomach. The victim recovered, but it proves that we should always be careful in preparing the food we eat.

ULTIMATE FACTS!

Marine worms of the *Anisakis simplex* family often infest raw fish. Human infection by these worms is called *anisakiasis*. This condition is most common in Scandinavia, Japan, the Netherlands, and South America — all countries where raw fish is regularly eaten.

Most Virulent Viral Disease

Record-holder:	Ebola hemorrhagic fever
Date:	1976 to present
Place:	Democratic Republic of the Congo

One of the world's most revolting diseases is also one of the deadliest. Ebola hemorrhagic fever (EHF), which first appeared in 1976 in Zaire (now the Democratic Republic of the Congo), kills up to 90 percent of its victims — a death tally that qualifies this killer for the title of **Most Virulent Viral Disease**. An Ebola infection starts in the form of a headache and fever, leads to massive internal and external bleeding, organ meltdown, and finally results in a total failure of the body's systems within days.

ULTIMATE FACTS!

Ebola hemorrhagic fever is rare. Only 2,305 victims and 1,525 deaths have been reported since the virus first emerged. The deadliest Ebola strain, Ebola-Zaire, kills nearly 90 percent of its victims. Other strains have a lower fatality rate.

Ebola Goes to the Movies

The 1995 movie *Outbreak* starring Dustin Hoffman and Morgan Freeman told the story of an Ebola-like virus striking a California town. Real life echoed fiction when the biggest-ever *real* Ebola outbreak struck the city of Kikwit, Zaire, during the movie's theater run. Officially, 315 people contracted Ebola and 250 died during the Kikwit epidemic, a death rate of 80 percent.

First Use of Forensic Entomology

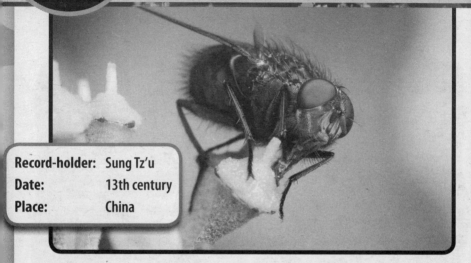

Record-holder:	Sung Tz'u
Date:	13th century
Place:	China

Did you know that ancient Chinese detectives used bugs? Not listening devices but *real* bugs! The **First Use of Forensic Entomology** was mentioned in a 13th-century Chinese textbook called *Hsi Yuan Lu* (The Washing Away of Wrongs) written by Sung Tz'u, a lawyer and death examiner. He describes the time he investigated a fatal stabbing in a rice field. No one confessed to the murder until he asked the workers to lay down their sickles. Soon, blowflies appeared and swarmed to one particular sickle, attracted by its then-invisible traces of blood. The worker confessed to the crime, and Sung Tz'u had made history in using entomology, or the scientific study of bugs, to solve a crime.

ULTIMATE FACTS!

Certain blowflies, particularly those of the species *Calliphora vomitoria* (pictured), prefer to lay their eggs in open wounds or fresh blood. The eggs hatch into larvae, which feast on the decayed matter surrounding them.

Most Detailed Human Dissection

Record-holder:	Visible Human Project
Date:	1994–95
Place:	Colorado, USA

The concept behind the Visible Human Project (VHP) is to create a virtual anatomy "textbook" for medical students to learn surgical techniques in the same way airplane pilots practice their flying skills on safely grounded flight simulators. This ambitious program required that the team slice a human corpse in the **Most Detailed Human Dissection** ever undertaken. Led by Dr. Victor Spitzer of the University of Colorado, the VHP released a "Visible Man" (with 1,871 slices) in 1994, and a "Visible Woman" (with 5,189 slices) in 1995. Every one of these slices was individually photographed and digitized to form the most precise anatomical database in medical history (pictured).

ULTIMATE FACTS!

The "Visible Man" is controversial. The body used to create this database was donated by a Death Row prisoner from Texas.

Most Common Skin Infection

Record-holder:	Athlete's foot
Place:	Worldwide

Watch your step! There's a fungus among us, and it may be lurking between your own toes. *Tinea pedis*, usually called "athlete's foot," is the **Most Common Skin Infection** in humans (pictured). This condition afflicts up to 70 percent of the worldwide population at any given moment, and almost everyone will feel the burn at least once in their lifetime. The fungus announces its repellent presence when the skin between the toes softens and peels away, and may start to crack and ooze. Feel familiar? If so, your feet may be hosting a record-breaker!

ULTIMATE FACTS!

The fungus that causes athlete's foot lives on damp floors, in wet towels, and inside sneakers. To avoid infection, don't let your bare feet touch these risk areas.

CHAPTER 4
An Original Odor

What's that smell? It's funky, foul, and a Guinness World Record-breaker! You'll be holding your nose when you read this chapter, although we're glad to say this book is not a scratch-and-sniff. We'll spotlight our planet's smelliest animals and substances, some naturally made while others are mixed up in beakers by chemists. Take a deep breath and get ready to smell everything from rotten meat to smelly feet.

Smelliest Plant

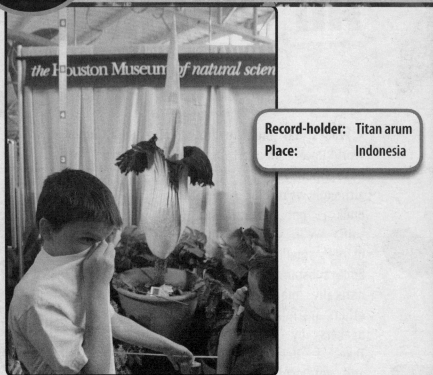

Record-holder: Titan arum
Place: Indonesia

Here's a showstopper at any flower show (pictured). Known as the world's **Smelliest Plant**, the titan arum (*Amorphophallus titanium*) emits an odor similar to rotting flesh when it blooms. The plant *looks* like dead meat, too. Its inner parts are warm — about human body temperature — and a blood-red color. Why would a plant mimic a slab of beef? It's because the "corpse flower," as the titan arum is nick-named, needs to attract meat-loving insects for pollination. The titan arum grows naturally in the rainforests of Sumatra. In the wild, it can reach heights of nearly 12 feet! A big titan arum is stinky enough to be smelled from a distance of at least half a mile. Beetles and flies are absolutely *buggy* about this Guinness World Record-holder!

Smelliest Mammal

Record-holder: Striped skunk
Place: Canada and continental USA

When it comes to B.O., one animal holds the top *rank*! The striped skunk (*Mephitis mephitis*), a member of the mustelid family, can eject a truly foul-smelling liquid from its anal glands (yes, we're talking about its butt) when it feels threatened. The reeking excretion is so potent that people can detect it at a concentration of 10 parts per billion. That's about the same dilution as a teaspoonful of milk stirred into an Olympic-sized swimming pool! Thanks to its super all-natural stench, the skunk earns the title of the world's **Smelliest Mammal** (pictured).

ULTIMATE FACTS!

Skunk spray contains seven compounds. Of these, the most powerful are two sulfur-based chemicals named *(E)-2-butene-1-thiol* and *3-methyl-1-butanethiol*. You'll need a long bath in tomato juice if you're exposed to either of these substances.

Smelliest Species of Frog

Record-holder:	Skunk frog
Date:	1991
Place:	Venezuela

Only a few specimens of the world's **Smelliest Species of Frog** (see illustration) have ever been found — but this sampling made a big impression on scientists' noses! The skin of the perfectly named Venezuelan skunk frog (*Aromabates nocturnus*) oozes a slimy substance that contains the same odor-producing chemicals as the spray of the **Smelliest Mammal**, the skunk. Like other (less stinky) members of the *Aromabates* family, the skunk frog releases its odorous ooze to defend itself. The creature's best safety strategy is in hiding. Researchers didn't discover it until 1991 and haven't found another specimen since 2005; therefore it is on the critically endangered species list.

ULTIMATE FACTS!

The Venezuelan skunk frog is the only nocturnal and aquatic member of its frog family. This means that it hunts only at night near rivers and streams.

Smelliest Bird

Record-holder: Hoatzin
Place: South American rainforests

The world's **Smelliest Bird** (pictured) has a stench that is guaranteed to ruffle your feathers! Native to the Colombian rainforest and the Amazon and Orinoco river basins, the odd-looking hoatzin (*Opisthocomus hoazin*) dines on green leaves, flowers, and fruits. It digests these materials through a cow-like fermentation process — and the result is a distinctly cow-like aroma. *Phew!* It's no wonder the locals nicknamed the hoatzin the *pava hedionda*, which translates as "stinking pheasant."

ULTIMATE FACTS!

Young hoatzin have two large claws on each wing. They use these claws to cling to tree branches until their wings develop and they learn how to fly.

Smelliest Cheese

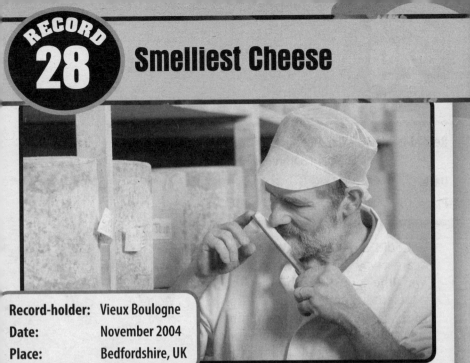

Record-holder:	Vieux Boulogne
Date:	November 2004
Place:	Bedfordshire, UK

An electronic nose and 19 human testers all agreed: When it comes to stinky cheese, a product called Vieux Boulogne is the winner! According to research conducted by Cranfield University in Bedfordshire, UK, in November 2004, Vieux Boulogne is the **Smelliest Cheese** (pictured) manufactured in the world. Made from cow's milk by Philippe Olivier of France, this malodorous morsel takes between seven and nine weeks to mature. During this time, enzymes in the cheese react to create the finished product's unique odor. You'd better hold your nose if someone serves this record-setting treat!

ULTIMATE FACTS!

Cheeses that lost out to Vieux Boulogne in Cranfield's whiff test included English cheddar, parmesan, and Epoisses de Bourgogne, a cheese so stinky that it is banned from public transportation in its native France.

Smelliest Substance

Record-holders: "Who-Me?" and "US Government Standard Bathroom Malodor"
Date: 1997
Place: Pennsylvania, USA

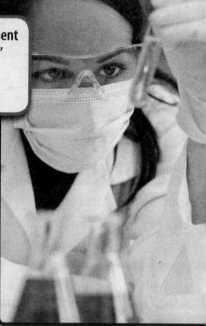

Could an extremely bad odor scare away your enemies? That was the question that led to a scientific sniff-test of "Who-Me?" and "US Government Standard Bathroom Malodor," two manmade smells that jointly hold the Guinness World Records title of **Smelliest Substance**. In 1997, these scents nosed out the competition in a study carried out at the Monell Chemical Senses Center in Philadelphia, Pennsylvania. "Who-Me?" contains five chemical ingredients while "Bathroom Malodor" has eight, yet it managed to nauseate people at a concentration of only *two parts per million*. "We got cursed in a lot of languages," laughs scientist Pam Dalton, who organized and conducted the rancid research (not pictured).

ULTIMATE FACTS!

"Who-Me?" smells strongly of human feces. "Bathroom Malodor" also has a fecal undertone, but adds the scents of spoiled eggs and rotting rodents to the final bouquet.

The Chemistry of Odor

Smells are created when molecules of a substance enter through your nostrils and drift up and back to a small patch the size of a postage stamp. This area contains your olfactory (smell) receptors. The molecules dissolve into the mucus inside your nose and connect with the receptors. Nerve endings "read" the molecules and transmit scent information to the brain. The brain then decides what it's smelling, and if the smell is good or — *phew* — bad. Everyone interprets odors differently, but two particular scents seem to be worse than others. *Ethyl mercaptan* (C_2H_5SH) and *butyl seleno-mercaptan* (C_4H_9SeH), which combine the aromas of rotting cabbage, garlic, onions, burnt toast, and sewer gas, seem to nauseate people of every age in every country worldwide.

Most Feet and Armpits Sniffed

Record-holder:	Madeline Albrecht
Date:	2000
Place:	Ohio, USA

Some people dislike their jobs, but here's a real stinker of a career! Madeline Albrecht worked as an "olfactory tester" also known as a professional sniffer at Hill Top Research Laboratories in Cincinnati, Ohio. Her duties included sniffing sweaty volunteers to test odor-reducing products under the Dr. Scholl brand. During her 15-year career at the lab, Madeline put her nose to the sniff-test against 5,600 feet and countless armpits, earning the title of **Most Feet and Armpits Sniffed** by the year 2000.

ULTIMATE FACTS!

Hill Top Research still conducts studies of personal care products. As of 2010, the company was recruiting volunteers to test dandruff shampoo, soap, moisturizers, sunscreens, toothpastes — and yes, underarm perspiration (pictured). Care to beat Madeline's record?

CHAPTER 5
What a Mouthful

When you invite certain Guinness World Record-holders to dinner, gastronomical grossness may result! This chapter pays lip service to the world's oddest diets, snacks, and mouthy measurements. See one man hold 400 straws in his mouth while another prefers a diet heavy in iron, starting with an airplane's parts. Fly to the next page and let's use our measuring tape to find out who has the biggest and bravest mouths in the world.

Widest Mouth

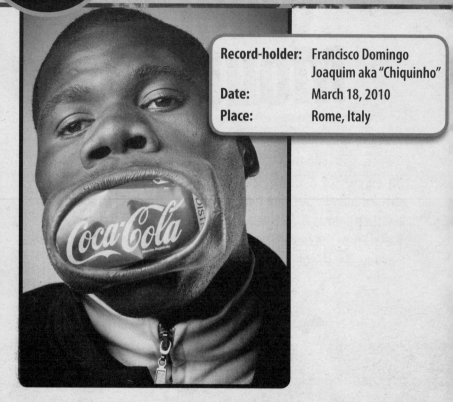

Record-holder:	Francisco Domingo Joaquim aka "Chiquinho"
Date:	March 18, 2010
Place:	Rome, Italy

This Guinness World Record-holder is a dentist's dream! Angola's Francisco Domingo Joaquim, who goes by the nickname "Chiquinho," can stretch his lips and cheeks to an unbelievable width of 6.69 inches. Chiquinho demonstrated his natural gifts on March 18, 2010, when his massive open-mouthed smile was officially measured on the set of *Lo Show dei Record* in Rome, Italy, and awarded the title of the world's **Widest Mouth** (pictured here and on this book's cover). To truly show the audience the width of his talent, Chiquinho inserted and removed a 12-ounce soda can from his mouth not once, not twice, but *14 times* in one minute.

Open Up

Chiquinho is the wide-mouth champion, but when it comes to top-to-bottom distance, an American thoroughly "licks" the competition! JJ Bittner can open his mouth to the **Largest Gape** ever measured in a human being. In full stretch, the space between JJ's upper and lower teeth is 3.4 inches. That's only a baby yawn in comparison to Africa's hippopotamus, the record-holder for the **Largest Mouth — Terrestrial Animal** (pictured). An adult male hippo can open its massive maw to almost 180 degrees, with an average distance of 4 feet!

RECORD 32

Widest Tongue

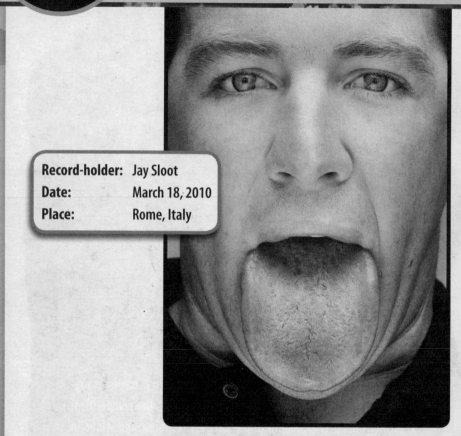

Record-holder:	Jay Sloot
Date:	March 18, 2010
Place:	Rome, Italy

Cat got your tongue? Guinness World Record-holder Jay Sloot would give any curious kitty plenty to catch! Jay, who hails from Australia, is the proud owner of the **Widest Tongue** ever measured on a human (pictured). A saliva-covered 3.1 inches from side to side, the awesome appendage made its first public appearance on March 18, 2010, on the set of *Lo Show dei Record* in Rome, Italy. Show producers really bit off a mouthful because this was the same episode when fellow record-holder Chiquinho made his impressive debut. Open wide!

Doggone It

Dogs are record-holders too, sometimes in the same categories as people. The record for **Longest Tongue on a Dog** belongs to Puggy (pictured). This male Pekingese is owned by Becky Stanford (both live in the USA). Puggy was 9 years old when his tongue set a new record-setting length at 4.5 inches. A veterinarian measured the dog's tongue from snout to tip three different times with the average measurement taken for record verification. Puggy said "Ahh" at Avondale Haslet Animal Clinic in Texas, USA, on May 8, 2009.

Largest Snail

Record-holder:	Gee Geronimo
Date:	December 1978
Place:	East Sussex, UK

This slimy record-holder can be a pet, a pest, or a meal, depending on which country it is found in. The African giant snail (*Achatina achatina*) is native to the forest floors of Ghana, West Africa. The **Largest Snail** ever measured was named Gee Geronimo (not pictured). In June 1976, Gee was collected from Sierra Leone, Africa, to become the pet of Christopher Hudson in Hove, East Sussex, UK. In December 1978, Gee's official record-setting measurements were 15.5 inches from snout to tail when fully extended, with a shell length of 10.75 inches, and a weight of 2 pounds.

ULTIMATE FACTS!

Also known as the giant Ghana or tiger snail, this gastropod is hunted by snail-pickers for dinner in Africa. In the USA, it is labeled as an invasive species capable of unbalancing the ecosystem.

Heaviest Spider

Record-holder: Rosi
Date: July 27, 2007
Place: Andorf, Austria

People are proud of their pets, whether a slimy snail or a hairy spider. Walter Baumgartner of Andorf, Austria, has a pet named Rosi who is the world's **Heaviest Spider** (pictured). Rosi is a female goliath bird-eating spider (*Theraphosa blondi*), a group famous for its shocking size and ability to stalk, pounce on, and eat many smaller animals including birds. But in South America, these giant spiders are served as a roasted treat. Good thing for Rosi she stayed in Austria for her record-setting measurements on July 27, 2007, with a weight of 6.17 ounces, a body length of 4.7 inches, a leg span of 10.2 inches, and a mandible of 0.9 inches.

ULTIMATE FACTS!

Goliath bird-eating spiders use hair for defense. The "hissing" sound or **stridulation** is the spider rubbing its bristly legs together before flicking its body hairs at its attacker. These hairs irritate a person's skin, especially around the eyes, nose, and mouth.

Most Big Macs® Eaten

Record-holder:	Donald Gorske
Date:	August 17, 2008
Place:	Wisconsin, USA

McDonald's Big Mac® hamburger packs a tasty but gut-busting punch that includes 540 calories, 30 grams of fat, and 1010 mg of sodium. Now multiply those numbers by 23,000 times. You're imagining the 37-year total achieved by Fond du Lac, Wisconsin, resident Donald Gorske, who holds the Guinness World Record for **Most Big Macs® Eaten** (pictured)! Donald enjoyed his first Big Mac® attack on May 17, 1972. He liked the experience so much that he repeated it for almost every day through August 17, 2008, when he reached his record-making milestone. "I need two to fill me up," Donald said in a 2008 interview.

ULTIMATE FACTS!

Donald Gorske keeps the receipts for every Big Mac® he has eaten, and his organizational skills made it easy to verify his Guinness World Records claim!

Leftovers Guaranteed

Feeling hungry for a BIG burger? Call 24 hours ahead of visiting Mallie's Sports Grill & Bar in Southgate, Michigan, to reserve your order for the world's **Largest Hamburger Commercially Available** (pictured). This burger weighed a jaw-dropping total of 185.8 pounds and cost $499 as of May 30, 2009. Better bring your friends and some extra take-home bags!

Strangest Diet

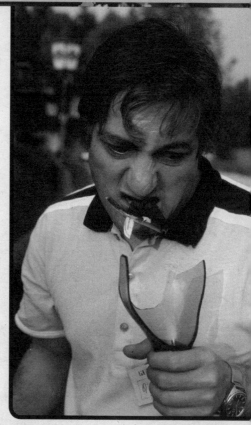

Record-holder:	Michel Lotito
Date:	1959
Place:	France

France is famous for its master chefs and fancy menus, offering exotic dishes with snails, frog legs, and other unusual cuisine (keep your eyes peeled for another food record set in France). A Frenchman named Michel Lotito from Grenoble, France, rose to fame outside of the kitchen. Also known as "Monsieur Mangetout" ("Mister Eats-All"), Michel had the unique ability to digest glass and metal (pictured). Starting in 1959 until his death in 2007, the man with the world's **Strangest Diet** ingested 18 bicycles, 15 supermarket carts, 7 TV sets, 6 chandeliers, 2 beds, a pair of skis, and a computer. He also ate a Cessna light aircraft and a coffin — handles and all. "It was empty; no one was inside," Michel was quick to explain in a 1998 article. X-rays revealed that Michel Lotito's stomach and intestinal linings were twice as thick as the average person. Thanks to his unusual anatomy, Michel could digest two pounds of metal every day. He could not, however, tolerate bananas and eggs. These foods were too soft for his metal-munching digestive system.

Most Prolific Cannibal

Record-holder:	Ratu Udre Udre
Date:	19th century
Place:	Fiji

In the 19th century, hordes of people were simply *dying* to join one Fijian chieftain for dinner — but not as honored guests. Between 872 and 999 humans were served as meals to Ratu Udre Udre, the **Most Prolific Cannibal** the world has ever recorded. Ratu's grisly gastronomical tally was preserved at the chief's gravesite in Rakiraki, northern Viti Levu, Fiji, where hundreds of stones — one for each victim — were placed next to the royal tomb. Talk about grisly record-keeping!

Most Straws Stuffed in the Mouth (Hands Off)

Record-holder: Simon Elmore
Date: August 6, 2009
Place: Bavaria, Germany

A successful comedian needs courage, confidence, lots of practice, and a big mouth, especially when you're the record-holder for **Most Straws Stuffed in the Mouth (Hands Off)**. Just ask British comedy performer Simon Elmore, when his mouth isn't full of drinking straws (pictured). Simon has been touring Europe with partner Mark Nicholas since 1979, when they formed the musical comedy act, "Mark'n'Simon." It was during their show on August 6, 2009, in Sollhuben, Bavaria, Germany, when Simon displayed his jaw-stretching skills. His personal goal was 402 straws, but he still set the record with 400 straws held in his mouth for 10 seconds without the use of his hands.

ULTIMATE FACTS!

The companion record **Most Straws Stuffed in the Mouth (Hands On)** belongs to Guinness Rishi, whose hands held 496 straws in his mouth for a total of 10 seconds on the set of *Guinness World Records — Ab India Todega* TV show in Mumbai, India, on March 17, 2011.

CHAPTER 6
Shocking Acts

We're nearly done with our excavation of the grossest records stored within the Guinness World Records archives. This chapter spotlights a collection of record-breaking actions, items, and incidents sure to surprise you in the best ways possible. You'll take a ride in a human-hair-covered car, toss some tomatoes during a massive food fight, feel the wind from the world's biggest whoopee cushion, and end your journey by getting slimed.

Largest Mammal to Explode, Forced

Record-holder:	Sperm whale
Date:	November 12, 1970
Place:	Oregon, USA

"Thar she blows!" These words summed up the situation on November 12, 1970, when a 16,000-pound, 45-foot-long sperm whale carcass washed up on the beach near Florence, Oregon (pictured). Not knowing quite how to dispose of their unwanted catch of the day, the Oregon State Highway Division decided to blast it to bits with 1,000 pounds of dynamite. The results were beyond anyone's wildest nightmares. Chunks of whale flew in every direction, raining down on spectators and vehicles up to ¼ mile away. The event set a record for the **Largest Mammal to Explode, Forced** — and it was a *whale* of a day for the Guinness World Records archives!

ULTIMATE FACTS!

Florence's exploding whale has passed into Oregon legend. Local residents retell the story, but most of them think it's a big fish tale. Every bit of this "tail" is 100 percent, certified true!

Pop Goes the Whale

The Oregon cetacean detonation was deliberate. A similar explosion in Taiwan, however, was completely natural. A sperm whale carcass measuring 55 feet 9 inches long and weighing 110,230 pounds was being removed, via truck bed, from the beach where it had washed up on January 26, 2004. In the heart of Tainan City, the cadaver blew to pieces due to a buildup of internal gases. Nearby pedestrians, vehicles, and shops were covered in the smelly, decomposing blubber and blood of the **Largest Mammal to Explode, Natural** (pictured).

Longest Surviving Headless Chicken

Record-holder:	Mike
Date:	September 10, 1945
Place:	Colorado, USA

"Fowl" is the only possible word to describe the story of Mike, a beheaded bird that holds the Guinness World Record for **Longest Surviving Headless Chicken** (pictured). Mike lost his head on September 10, 1945, when owner Lloyd Olsen of Fruita, Colorado, decided to butcher the robust rooster. Imagine Lloyd's surprise when Mike refused to die and tried to peck the ground with his neck stump instead! Bowing to Mike's incredible will to live, Lloyd kept the animal alive for another 18 months by dripping liquid food directly into its gaping gullet. It was a yucky job, but Lloyd could handle it — he was no chicken.

ULTIMATE FACTS!

The town of Fruita honors its now-deceased headless celebrity each year with a festival called "Mike the Headless Chicken Day." Events include Chicken Bingo, a Headless Chicken Race, and a "Pin the Head on the Chicken" contest.

Hairiest Car

Record-holder:	Marialucia Mugno
Date:	March 4, 2010
Place:	Rome, Italy

Here's a vehicle with a truly unique style — HAIRstyle, that is! Italian hairdresser Marialucia Mugno decided to give her car a makeover. She added a furry pelt of human hair, inside and out, to her 1975 Fiat 500. She imported about 220 pounds of hair from India to complete the automotive tress-up dress-up. The result was the world's **Hairiest Car** (pictured), which was unveiled on the set of *Lo Show dei Record* in Rome, Italy, on March 4, 2010. It was a good hair day for Marialucia and her car.

ULTIMATE FACTS!

Marialucia Mugno is famous in Italy for her hair creations. She has made human-hair clothing, violins, hats, and even a sculpture of the Eiffel Tower!

A Must-"Sea" Hairdo

While we're on the subject of unexpectedly hairy objects, let's take a quick saltwater dip to marvel at the world's **Furriest Fish** (see illustration). *Mirapinna esau*, a 2.5-inch resident of the mid-Atlantic Ocean, is covered with furlike growths instead of scales. Does that sound like a fish tale? It isn't! Scientists pulled the hairy critter from the water about 547 miles north of the Azores in 1911. No one knows exactly what *Mirapinna esau*'s "fur" does, and because scientists can't find another specimen, they aren't likely to find out anytime soon. This fish was "hair" today, gone tomorrow!

Largest Annual Food Fight

Record-holder:	La Tomatina
Date:	August 2004
Place:	Spain

"Food fight!" This cafeteria cry hits the streets each August in Buñol, Spain, a small city that is home to the world's **Largest Annual Food Fight** (pictured). La Tomatina, as the event is called, is a slippery skirmish that encourages people to pelt each other with freshly squished tomatoes. In 2004, around 38,000 people flung 275,500 pounds of tomatoes at each other within the span of one hour to set a new Guinness World Record. By the end of the tomato-tastic affair, the participants and the streets ran red with tomato juice, in some places as deep as 12 inches! Luckily, fire trucks were on hand to hose down everything and everyone.

ULTIMATE FACTS!

La Tomatina begins with a ham being hoisted up a greased pole. The tomato fight cannot start until someone slithers up the pole and frees the ham. Cannon fire alerts the crowd when someone has grabbed the ham and the tomato-tossing can start.

Oldest Vomit

Record-holder:	Ichthyosaur fossil
Date:	February 12, 2002
Place:	Peterborough, UK

About 160 million years ago, a large marine reptile called an ichthyosaur lost its lunch. Through the centuries, the prehistoric puke hardened into a fossil and survived the elements to be discovered by a team of paleontologists led by Professor Peter Doyle from Greenwich University, UK (pictured). They found the world's **Oldest Vomit** in a Peterborough, UK, quarry on February 12, 2002. The scientific community greeted the discovery with great excitement. You learn a lot about any animal by studying its diet, including the leftovers. Scientists hope that the fossil will "cough up" more details about the feeding habits of ichthyosaurs.

ULTIMATE FACTS!

The **Oldest Vomit** contains the remains of dozens of belemnites. Hordes of these squid-like shellfish once lived in the area that is now Great Britain.

Repulsed

What's the most repulsive sound you've ever heard? This nasty noise beat out fingernails scratching a chalkboard, a dentist's drill, and microphone feedback among others to earn the title of **Worst Sound to the Human Ear** on January 24, 2007. A yearlong, online survey run by Trevor Cox, Professor of Acoustic Engineering at Salford University, UK, discovered that someone vomiting was the auditory champ. The University's Acoustic Research Centre analyzed more than 1.1 million votes from international visitors to the BadVibes website (www.sound101.org).

Largest Whoopee Cushion

Record-holder:	Steve Mesure
Date:	June 14, 2008
Place:	London, UK

When Steve Mesure of the UK felt a good idea coming on, he decided to let it rip! Steve is the proud designer/ manufacturer of a whoopee cushion measuring 10 feet in diameter. That's the **Largest Whoopee Cushion** the world has ever seen (pictured)! It was displayed on June 14, 2008, at the Street Vibe sound festival in London, UK. Volunteers were encouraged to sit on the enormous air bag to demonstrate how wind instruments work. We're not sure we want to listen to any orchestra that uses *this* gross gadget!

ULTIMATE FACTS!

The modern whoopee cushion was invented by employees of the JEM Rubber Company in Toronto, Canada, in 1930. The indelicate item went on to become one of the most popular gag gifts of all time.

First Game to be Controlled by the Player's Posterior

Record-holder: Rayman Raving Rabbids TV Party

Date: November 18, 2008

Now here's an activity that inspired record-breakers can really get behind! "Rayman Raving Rabbids TV Party," a Wii™ game released first in Europe on November 18, 2008, is described by publisher Ubisoft as "the first video game you can play with your butt." To control a minigame segment called "Beestie Boarding" (pictured), players sit on a Wii balance board™ accessory and shift their weight left and right to steer their virtual character. Want to try the **First Game to be Controlled By the Player's Posterior**? You'd better have a talented tushie!

ULTIMATE FACTS!

"Rayman Raving Rabbids TV Party" was nominated for a "Best Use of Balance Board" award in 2008. It lost by a *hare* to "Wii Fit™," a home-fitness program.

Most People Simultaneously Slimed

Record-holder:	*Slimetime Live*
Date:	October 27, 2003
Place:	Florida, USA

A total of 762 people found themselves in a sticky situation on October 27, 2003, when they volunteered to become the subjects of the Guinness World Record for **Most People Simultaneously Slimed** (not pictured). The massive glop drop, which required 150 gallons of green goo, took place during Nickelodeon Studios' *Slimetime Live* show at Universal Studios in Orlando, Florida. The slime was fired into the air by 10 cannons. It then rained back down onto the delighted crowd. We bet this stunt got lots of "ooze" and ahhhs from the audience!

ULTIMATE FACTS!

Nickelodeon wanted to slime 1,000 people for its Guinness World Record attempt, but *Slimetime Live* producers couldn't find enough volunteers. They had to settle for the still-winning total of 762 instead.

CONCLUSION
Get Grosser

Our profile of the ultimate gross record-breakers ends here, but you can "get grosser" by continuing to discover more astonishing feats and facts in the online archives (*www.guinnessworldrecords. com*) and within the pages of *Guinness World Records* at your local library or bookstore. You're guaranteed to find thousands of records covering all things slimy and smelly, large and loud, plus many other measurements to overwhelm your senses.

Interested in making history by having your own record? Check out the official guidelines featured on the next page on how you can become a record-breaker. Maybe your name will appear in the next edition of the record book!

Be a Record-breaker

Message from the Keeper of the Records:

Record-breakers are the ultimate in one way or another — the youngest, the oldest, the tallest, the smallest. So how do you get to be a record-breaker? Follow these important steps:

1. Before you attempt your record, check with us to make sure your record is suitable and safe. Get your parents' permission. Next, contact one of our officials by using the record application form at *www.guinnessworldrecords.com*.

2. Tell us about your idea. Give us as much information as you can, including what the record is, when you want to attempt it, where you'll be doing it, and other relevant information.

a) We will tell you if a record already exists, what safety guidelines you must follow during your attempt to break that record, and what evidence we need as proof that you completed your attempt.

b) If your idea is a brand-new record nobody has set yet, we need to make sure it meets our requirements. If it does, then we'll write official rules and safety guidelines specific to that record idea and make sure all attempts are made in the same way.

3. Whether it is a new or existing record, we will send you the guidelines for your selected record. Once you receive these, you can make your attempt at any time. You do not need a Guinness World Record official at your attempt. But you do need to gather evidence. Find out more about the kind of evidence we need to see by visiting our website.

4. Think you've already set or broken a record? Put all of your evidence as specified by the guidelines in an envelope and mail it to us at Guinness World Records.

5. Our officials will investigate your claim fully — a process that can take a few weeks, depending on the number of claims we've received and how complex your record is.

6. If you're successful, you will receive an official certificate that says you are now a Guinness World Record-holder!

Need more info? Check out *www.guinnessworldrecords.com* for lots more hints, tips, and some top record ideas. Good luck!

PHOTO CREDITS

The publisher would like to thank the following for their kind permission to use their photographs in this book:

4-5, 78-80 Detail of a group of Zophobas morio © werg/Shutterstock; 6 Grouse © Peggi Miller/iStockphoto; 9 Boy sticking out tongue, 49 Cheese-maker, 77 Girl sticking out tongue © Media Bakery RF; 10-11 Tommy Mattinson, 23 Andrew Dahl, 54 Francisco Domingo Joaquim, 56 Jay Sloot, 57 Puggy, 58 Snail © Paul Michael Hughes/Guinness World Records; 13 Garry Turner, 19 Kim Goodman, 60 Donald Gorske © Drew Gardner/Guinness World Records; 14 Rob Williams © Michelle Bates www.michellebates.net; 15 Rob Williams © Brenda Ladd Photography www.brendaladdphoto.com; 16 Michele Forgione, 26 Kevin Cole © Guinness World Records; 17 Paul Hunn © Ranald Mackechnie/Guinness World Records; 18 Map of Italy © fzd.it/Shutterstock; 20 The Space Cowboy © Chayne Hultgren/Guinness World Records; 21 (top) Dong Changsheng © China Photos/Getty Images; 21 (bottom) Thomas Blackthorne, 64 Simon Elmore, 69 Hairiest Car © John Wright/Guinness World Records; 24 Ilker Yilmaz © Osman Orsal/AP Photo; 25 Nasal diagram © John Bavosi/SPL/Photo Researchers; 27 Boy with wormy apple © Peter Menzel www.menzelphoto.com; 28 Hagfish © Tom McHugh/Photo Researchers, Inc.; 29 Hookworm © David Scharf/Science Faction/Corbis; 30 Tick engorged © David Wrobel/Visuals Unlimited/Corbis; 31 Tick warning sign © lantapix/Shutterstock; 32 Roundworm © Sinclair Stammers/Photo Researchers, Inc.; 33 Leech © Caters News/ZUMA Press; 34 Broad tapeworm © Darlyne A. Murawski/National Geographic/Getty Images; 34 (inset) Tapeworm eggs © CNRI/Photo Researchers, Inc.; 35 Mad doctor © Nina Malyna/Shutterstock; 36 Casu Marzu © Shardan/Wikimedia Commons; 37 Sashimi © svry/Shutterstock; 38 Health workers © Ho New/Reuters; 39 Kikwit hospital © Corinne Dufka/Reuters; 40 Blowfly © J.J. Harrison/Wikimedia Commons; 41 VHP © University of Colorado Health Sciences Center/AP Photo; 42 Athlete's foot © SPL/Photo Researchers, Inc.; 43 Boy with stinky shoe © José Manuel Gelpi Díaz/Alamy RF; 44 Boy smells the titan arum © Richard Carson/Reuters; 45 Titan arum © Tony Larkin/Rex USA; 46 Striped skunk © Tom Brakefield/Stockbyte/Getty Images RF; 47 Venezuelan skunk frog art © Joseph Trumpey/Michigan Science Art; 48 Hoatzin © Morales Morales/AGE/Photolibrary; 50 Female lab worker © Darren Baker/Shutterstock; 51 Chemistry art © Rocket400 Studio/Shutterstock; 52 Odor testing at Hill Top Research Laboratories © AP Photo; 53 Yelling child © Larry Lilac/Alamy RM; 55 Hippo © Timothy Craig Lubcke/Shutterstock; 59 Rosi © Richard Bradbury/Guinness World Records; 61 Largest Hamburger © Larry Caruso; 62 Monsieur Mangetout © Rex USA; 63 Dinner setting © Cico/Shutterstock; 65 Woman slimed; 76 Child slimed © Nicole Hill/Rubberball/AGE Fotostock; 66 Sperm whale beached © Robin Bush/OSF/Getty Images; 67 Tainan City © STR/AFP/Getty Images; 68 Mike © Bob Landry/Time Life Pictures/Getty Images; 70 Furriest Fish art © Brian Cressman/Michigan Science Art; 71 La Tomatina © Fernando Vergara/AP Photo; 72 Oldest Vomit © University of Greenwich; 73 Boy clasping ears © Huron Photo/iStockphoto; 74 Largest Whoopee Cushion © Mykel Nicolau/Guinness World Records; 75 Beestie Boarding image © Ubisoft